WRITING
FOR
PLEASURE

MICHAEL ROSEN

Introduction

This is the third booklet in a series I've written for teachers, students and anyone involved in reading, writing and oracy with school students of all ages.

In the first, *Poetry and Stories for Primary and Lower Secondary Schools*, I have some suggestions for writing poetry and analysing pupils' responses to any form of literature. In the second, *Why Read? Why Write?*, I've made suggestions for how to analyse texts using a broad range of methods and I offered some ways of justifying creative work in the classroom for teachers who are meeting resistance against this kind of work.

In this booklet I am outlining a process for helping pupils enjoy writing.

I hope any of the three booklets (or all three!) can be used by teachers and others as a basis for classroom work or as a focus for in-service training and discussion.

They are all available through my website.

Visit 'Books' at michaelrosen.co.uk

Part 1

We often talk about reading for pleasure – good thing too – but in a way writing for pleasure is harder, and, I think, happens less often.

Why would that be?

Most of us learn to talk without anyone teaching us. It happens because we are around other people talking and if it was hard or odd or confusing, we can't remember it being like that, because we learnt how to do most of it in a time we can't recall. Writing, on the other hand, is something that we are taught and most of us can remember a few things about times when we were being taught.

I can remember most of my teachers telling me that I had terrible handwriting, other teachers telling me that I was 'good at writing even though my handwriting was terrible'. I can also remember my dad giving me advice on how to write – he was a secondary school teacher and the advice he gave me was: write about what you know and don't try to write about what you don't know. (I think he was talking about writing non-fiction essays and realistic stories, not fantasy!)

One reason – I think it's the main one – that writing is hard is because there are various things about it that are very different from the way we speak to each other.

When we speak to each other we do many of the following things that we tend not to do when we write:

- make gestures, such as pointing to people and things
- interrupt ourselves and other people
- not finish what we seemed to be going to say
- letting other people finish what we were going to say
- hesitating
- speeding up and slowing down
- being more or less musical in the way we string words together
- stressing parts of words, whole words and phrases (though we can do this a bit in writing by using italics and capital letters)
- repeating words, phrases and sentences
- using a lot of phrases like 'you know' or 'like'
- doing a lot of 'umming and erring'
- use a lot of 'pronouns' without saying who the 'he', 'she', 'it', 'we' or 'they' actually are because we are assuming that other people listening know who we're talking about
- saying things in a way that is 'compressed' or 'contracted' like 'I'd've' (though some of these we can write down, just as I've written 'I'd've'!)
- using regional, local and non-standard words and phrases
- and – not talking in the long, sentences that we use when we write!

When we write, a lot – but by no means all – of the writing we do is not organised in the way we organise language in speech.

In continuous prose (the kind of writing I'm doing now), we mostly organise things into sentences, and if it's standard English, this means that most of the sentences have a full verb in the middle of it, which has a 'subject'. This is the main 'axis' or 'elbow' of a sentence. (The last sentence you've just read, that axis was 'This is . . .' 'This' is the 'subject' and 'is' (in this case) was the full verb or 'finite verb' as some people call it.

When we speak, we quite often don't organise our speech into 'subject verb' sentences.

When we write, we have to explain every pronoun, or people won't know who or what we are talking about.

When we write we can make sentences grow, particularly if we revise what we write. We can add extra phrases that begin with words like 'in', 'on', 'by', 'with'. We can add extra clauses that begin with words like 'although', 'because', 'if', 'as soon as', 'when', 'where', 'who', 'that'. We can link one idea to another using 'and',or 'but'. We can of course use all these words, phrases and clauses when we speak. What I'm saying here is that when we write, we can lever in more of them, making what we mean more complicated.

Another thing we can do is what the linguist David Crystal calls, 'front-loading' a sentence. When we speak, we tend to dive straight into that 'subject-verb' thing, or even straight into the verb.

'What you doing?

'Going out.'

If I was reporting that I would write, 'She asked me what I was doing, and I said that I was going out.'

That's a very different 'construction' of language. I can also, add in things at the front about when and where I was when 'she' asked me what I was doing. I can also say some things about 'she'. I can, if I choose, put some of these up front, in a way that I might find difficult when speaking.

'In a room that was neither a pub or a shop but had the air of being a bit of both, she asked me what I was doing . . .'

Some people can speak like that – especially stand-up comedians, politicians, and in the kind of rehearsed, written speech that you get in plays and films or people like me reading off scripts on the radio.

Most of the time, we don't talk like that.

Both talking and writing take place over longer stretches of time than a single sentence or just a few sentences. We might chat for hours. We can write things that take hours or even days to read. How these two ways of using language are organised are very different too. When you look at transcripts of people talking for a time, there is often a 'circularity'. People give each other accounts of things, and often come back to them, sometimes again and again. They also signal to each other that in many different ways things that indicate they are listening to each other ('Mm', 'Go on', 'Really?'), they indicate when they are bored, when they haven't followed what the other persons is saying, and various kinds of comments about whether the conversation should go on, wind up soon, or wind up now!

In writing, we hardly use any of these. In fact, part of the oddness of writing is that we do it without anyone saying, 'Mm' or 'Go on,' or 'Right . . . OK then . . .' We do it to and for a silent audience. This simple fact is one of the main reasons why writing is difficult. We have to imagine our audience, we have to 'internalise' an audience (that is, write for that audience without saying we are), and every word and phrase and sentence we use, does in fact 'imply' an audience. This is because in a way, everything we say and write comes from stores of language (words, phrases, sentences, etc.) which are a bit like shelves in libraries: stores of language for particular reasons and purposes, waiting for us to use, adapt and re-use. When we speak or write about, say, the kind of car we want to get, we go to the car shelf and start talking in a kind of car dialect. This is much easier when we speak because the person we're speaking to might well help us. When we write, we have to do it with no help. So, when we're writing about, say, 'The Tudors', we have to go to the history shelf and pull down the 'history way of writing' and there isn't anyone to prompt us with words and phrases that historians use, like 'on the other hand . . .' or 'another problem that Elizabeth faced . . .' We have to learn these in order to be the kind of person who can write like that. Again, it's not easy!

In writing, we can 'develop an argument' or 'structure a plot' or organise a poem according to a fixed form like a sonnet or a ballad, There are then 'strings' that run through pieces of writing that are, say, the way we organise a series of 'points' in an argument, discussion or 'exploration of a theme'. There might be 'strings' which guide us in shaping a whole song or poem, and there might be rhythms to the length of scene or the kinds of dialogue that we put in a play which again are a bit like invisible strings holding and shaping the whole piece of writing. Incredibly rare and clever people can do some or even most of this when they talk. In fact, it's easier for most of us to do this when we have time to think and 'draft' and 'redraft' our writing!

We might say, then, that the kinds of writing I'm talking about here (continuous prose, poems and other forms of literature) are a bit like a dialect that is different from the one that we speak with. It's not a perfect analogy, but if I stick with it for a moment: consider trying to speak with the dialect you don't speak with. In my case that would be, say, Glaswegian. Immediately I'm thinking of things like 'canna' and 'dinna', the Glaswegian way of saying the kind of things that I say as 'can't' and 'don't'. I have to learn those words in order to say them. That's a bit (not totally) like the process by which we learn to write in standard English continuous prose. And it's not easy, particularly when we're very young, and particularly when we're both learning how to physically form words with our pencils and pens at the same time as learning this new way of using English.

The question, then, is how do we make all this pleasurable?

However, before getting into this, I'll need to explore the question of different kinds of writing. One of the ways in which we 'mystify' writing is to tell children and adults that really there is only one way to write – standard English, continuous prose.

In fact, there are many, many different ways of writing and even within some forms of standard English continuous prose – like, say, in novels, or newspapers, where there are loads of times when it's not very standard, and not very 'continuous'. Here are some types of writing that are like this:

TV and film scripts, plays, poems, songs, TV ads, posters, newspaper headlines, slogans, dialogue in novels, the words in a children's picture book, emails, texts, comments in social media, shopping lists, labels, some instructions.

Let's never forget that all this writing is important, a lot of it is a crucial part of how we enjoy ourselves, get things done, and in some cases make money!

This is why that anyone teaching writing knows that one way to make writing pleasurable is to do some of it in these ways, even if it's only in a kind of mock way – 'let's make up a mock ad for toenails'. This is then a kind of 'bridging' place to get writing going, which is neither speech, nor standard English continuous prose.

It's 'something else' and, as it happens, it's a territory I've been exploring for about the last 50 years or more: writing in ways that make the writing 'easy to say out loud' and I do this in most of my poetry, in my radio scripts and in a good deal of my stories and some of my blogs – even this one that you've just read.

Part 2

Here is a short list of principles or processes which we can use to help us to write for pleasure:

Collecting, investigating, imitating, changing (or inventing), distributing.

(One important aspect of this list is that we should think of it as interconnected: each process feeds into another. For example (and I'll return to this) 'distributing' is as important as any other process on the list because how people react when something is 'distributed' feeds back into what and how we write. It's how we put 'audience' into our writing. I mention this interconnectedness because it's very easy to pull one of these elements out and just focus on it, hoping that it'll do the trick.)

By the way, this is not just about 'creative writing' and it's not just about 'continuous prose'. It's about all kinds of writing. More on that later.

Collecting:

'Out there', every day, there are millions of examples of 'language-use' – spoken and written. We can think of it as a resource, which we can use to pick and mix, or 'scavenge' for what we want from it. This is what I mean by collecting.

Investigating:

The moment we have collected a 'specimen' of language-use – it can be anything from a single word, to a whole book; anything from a line for a song, a comment that someone made to a whole speech or a play – we can investigate it. We can look at it and ask it questions about why it is the way it is, how it works, why we are interested in it, why we are/are not moved by it and so on.

Imitating:

Any piece of language-use can be imitated, copied, repeated. So long as it's not a burden, this has the advantage of putting that sequence of words into our minds and bodies, with all its rhythms and strategies.

Changing or inventing:

Any piece of language-use that we are imitating, can be played about with, tinkered with. The more we do this, the more confident we become with writing. There is, if you like, a scale of kinds of change: at one end, there are tiny changes, at the other there are huge changes, some so big that it's almost impossible to see what is being imitated. At this end of the scale the original text is really a 'trigger' which leads to big inventions.

Distributing:

Any piece of writing can be seen as a piece of language-use that can be distributed – that is shared through the means of using digital media (blogs (e.g., quadblogging), school websites, bulletins, fan fiction etc.); 'old' media – booklets, posters, letters, magazines, ; performances – to one other person, a group, a class, a whole school, a parents' evening, a local community event, a video, a PowerPoint show and so on.

In the following sections, I'll go through each of these processes in turn with ideas on how to do these, bearing in mind (again) that the list is intended to be interconnected so that each process can help the others.

Part 3

Collecting Language

'Out there', every day, there are millions of examples of 'language-use' – spoken and written. We can think of it as a resource, which we can use to pick and mix, or 'scavenge' for what we want from it. This is what I mean by collecting.

I. Speech: It's great to focus children and school students on their own speech and the speech of the people they hear around them, relatives' sayings, proverbs, aphorisms, slips of the tongue, things they hear in the institutions they go through (school, hospital etc.) and what they hear on holiday or on the media. We can create spaces on walls, in books, or in corners, where we collect whatever is interesting, ambiguous, odd, fantastic, muddled, funny, tragic, pithy, clever, enigmatic. Teachers can model this by bringing in a few examples from e.g., their parents, off the TV, toddler talk, overheard on the bus, etc., in order to get things going.

This is what many writers do. It's a writing activity. The key thing is to keep it refreshed and enriched, so maybe you have to keep changing it, every month or so.

Encourage children and students to use it, to create their own versions of it. By 'use' it I mean that we can draw attention to items on the list and discuss them.

2. Writing: The same goes for examples of writing. This can include anything from poems, stories, plays that are being read, ads seen on buses or on posters, things taken from newspapers, odd things from text books,good jokes from joke books, stuff clipped from magazines. Again, the principle is 'clipping'. It can include lines from songs, street signs, odd things written on products, instructions for furniture you have to assemble, recipes – any examples of writing that catch the eye.

It can also include the idea of 'anthologising'. Encourage children and students to make anthologies of passages of writing they like or are intrigued by or puzzled by. It doesn't have to be marked or overseen. You can set it for homework, just copy anything, a few quotes, a passage that appeals to you, a verse from a song in the charts. And you can encourage the pupils to talk about the pieces, (perhaps in a designated time) or by writing a few words about it in their anthologies.

Again, many writers do this.

All of this are ways of making how language works, explicit. It draws attention to the way in which we are affected by language in many different ways.

It is also non-hierarchical. It says that language is everywhere, in use, affecting us whether it's 'popular', 'mass media', 'high art', 'commercial'; whether it's 'perfect' or an error, slip of the tongue, ambiguity, pun, piece of rhetoric or some such. All this is scope for discussion and contributes to 'knowledge about language'. It may well uncover how language works on affecting us.

3. Collecting longer kinds of writing: Essentially this means a library! We have to ask ourselves how pupils get access to the huge variety of written text in the world: school library, local library, internet, theatre, film, and all the ways in which text is blasted at us through TV, ads, promos, captions and so on.

If we want pupils to write, we have to, bit by bit, get them interested in saying – in broad or specific terms – 'I would like to write like that'. Essentially, this is what Shakespeare said to himself when he sat down to write his sonnets. It is part and parcel of a writer's job, to say, 'I would like to write like that'. This can mean, 'using that form', or it can mean 'trying to express those ideas'. or 'using that motif', 'using that theme' or indeed, 'something triggered off by what I just read'.

One of the best ways to understand form, theme, structure, genre is quite simply, 'trying to write like that'. By creating a pseudo-science of 'analysis' we have made it hard for ourselves. It is really much easier to have a go ourselves.

However, if we are just 'set the task' of doing this, it can be off-putting. If we've collected an example, and imitate the example we like or are interested in, it's usually a much more motivated task.

At the heart off all this, is the motor of 'making literacy mine'. One of the jobs of education is not simply to say, 'we are endowing pupils with this chunk of literature' but it is to find ways for the notion of literacy to be one of possession. 'I, the pupil, have the right to own this piece of writing, or this kind of writing. It doesn't belong to one person, or to one kind of person, or to one institution – but to everyone. And I am part of everyone, so I'm entitled to have this and use this.'

That message is particularly important for those who get a sense that some or all writing doesn't belong to them.

Collecting examples of speech and writing, talking about it, making anthologies carried with those activities, the message that it all belongs to you.

Part 4

Investigating

The guiding principle for most of the government's guidelines on how to investigate or explore language and literature is that we have to follow the methods laid down in the tests and exams. These include: breaking words down into sounds, words given names for the 'class' of words they belong to, words given 'functions' in sentences, words and phrases given 'good' places for them to go in sentences, some words and types of phrases elevated to being better than others, the processes of 'retrieval', 'inference', 'chronology' and 'presentation' being decided upon as the sole criteria for comprehension.

As a collection of practices, they add up to a view of 'language in education' that all that is worth knowing about language belongs to 'education' and if you want to know anything about language or language in literature and writing, the only way to know it is by being taught or instructed.

The point is that there are other approaches which can be mixed with the government approved methods, can on occasions precede them, can on occasions be used instead of them.

The alternative starting point is to think of language, language in literature, language in all kinds of writing, as a phenomenon just as we might treat, say, 'the sea' or 'energy'. That's to say, we can 'learn about it' in several different ways, one of which is to investigate it, explore it, discuss it. Prior to doing that, we have to 'sample' it, and in Writing for Pleasure 3, I described some ways of collecting language, some of which is pupil-led. Of course, of course, of course (!) collection that is pupil-led can be mingled with what is teacher-led (providing of texts, quotes, songs, poems, stories, plays etc.).

(Irony: in the 1950s, there was an assumption that the job of schools was to provide pupils with 'Literature' – poems, stories and plays. I'm hearing from teachers that there are key times in e.g., in the primary curriculum, when on occasions, usually prior to Key Stage 1 and 2 SATs, senior management will query or even ban e.g., poetry, or 'free reading'. I've heard of schools that more or less dispensed with books in class but have followed e.g., Ruth Miskin's course of extract and exercises instead.)

In my *Poetry and Stories for Primary and Lower Secondary Schools* and *What is Poetry?* I've outlined a basic way in which any piece of language from any source can be investigated. ('Any piece' can mean words, phrases, sentences, passages, chapters, poems, scenes or whole books – quite literally – any). These are for teachers and parents and pupils to adapt and change depending age and circumstances. I summarise them here:

1. Probing ways in which the example 'reminds' you of anything in your life, or the lives of anyone you know. How? Why?

2. Probing ways in which the example 'reminds' you of any other 'text' (film, story, song, TV programme, poem, etc.). How? Why?

3. Are there any questions you would like to ask anyone IN the example? Any questions you would like to ask the author? Can you answer any of those questions yourself. If you can't, what do you need to do to answer them?

4. In every piece of writing – especially poetry – there are 'secret strings' which link one part to another. These can be strings that link sounds, rhythms, repetitions, patterns. They can be strings that link 'images', rhetorical devices, structures of sentences. They can be strings that link by means of e.g., opposites (or 'binaries') or 'series' e.g., threes. We can be 'detectives' (younger children enjoy this), and hunt for these strings. We can then discuss what are these strings for? Why has the author created them? What effect do they have?

In my experience, the best way to structure a class around these questions is to vary between talk in twos, and whole class. You can research what pupils are getting from this experience ('learning outcome' !) by making recordings of samples of their talk, transcribing them and using the 'matrix' I've put in *Poetry and Stories for Primary and Lower Secondary Schools* to analyse what is going on. (This is what we do on the MA in Children's Literature at Goldsmiths.)

The pupils' questions, discussions and answers are themselves a resource for writing. They will involve the pupils' lives, queries, matters of interest, thoughts about a range of texts from outside the classroom, questions of structure, intention, choice of words, images, phrases, sounds. Some of the answers may involve e.g., 'hot seating' (if, say, someone answers a question for an author or a character etc.).

Any of these can be starting points for writing. Teachers have told me that if they go through these four stages, quite often they haven't had to set something to write about, the pupils have asked to 'write something like that' or some such, straightaway.

Or, of course, we can 'grab' something that someone has said, (or the way they've said it and suggest that.

Part 5

Imitating

I have no snobberies or fears about imitation.

The simplest way to think about this is to see every piece of writing as something that is available to us to imitate or copy. The question that hangs over this, is to what extent do we as writing-teachers point things out about what it is being copied?

For example, we might look at how a series of story-writers begin stories, begin chapters, begin scenes. We could say, 'let's copy that', meaning let's copy that way of doing things. We could also ask, are there any guidelines here about the way story-writers begin things? The author Morris Gleitzman and present Children's Laureate in Australia, once told me that he likes to begin any book and any scene, 'as late as I can'. What he meant is that he didn't like to use up any words setting up a scene, he liked to get straight into some action or dialogue.

Another example: how does writing do 'reveal-conceal'? It is essential to all writing because you can't say everything at once. In fact, quite often in nearly all writing, we flag up that we've got more to write, or there's more to come, or there's something mysterious, dangerous, exciting etc., about to happen or will happen later – and so on. These reveal-conceal moments are often the 'hook' that helps to pull us through a piece of writing. Note: I don't just mean in fiction. Think, even a recipe has reveal-conceals – we write 'Ingredients'. That's an invitation to go on reading. Newspapers do it with headlines which indicate something serious or absurd has happened without telling you how. Even the single word 'disaster' is a reveal-conceal until we know what the nature of the disaster is.

Another example: how is a piece of writing 'narrated'? Who is the narrator, who is being narrated to? Does this change across a paragraph? Chapter? Across a book, or newspaper or magazine? This business of narration is a crucial aspect of how a piece of writing has meaning and how its ideas are expressed.

Another: how are thoughts conveyed? A good deal of writing, fiction and non-fiction has to use ready-made ways of saying what is thought, what is opinion, who is having these thoughts or opinions. In non-fiction we have to decide when it's valid or OK to say that an opinion comes from the writer – or not. In fiction, we have to decide whose mind are we going to hear about? Everyone's? The main character's?

Another: most stories put characters into situations in which they have problems or dilemmas, they face jeopardy or peril, they succeed in overcoming this in stages, sometimes with setbacks, sometimes with help, sometimes hindered or distracted (because the author deliberately tries to throw the reader off the scent of being able to predict the ending), until there is some sort of resolution.

Another: how is time represented? Most writing conveys time frames in which what's being told, sits. However, quite a lot of writing mentions events past and future, and it can also convey the idea of 'continuous time' in the sense that there is a state of being that is continuous, e.g., 'she had brown eyes', or there was a continuous state of being in the past, 'he used to wear a brown hat'. It's interesting to see how the time frames stay constant and/ or change in a piece of writing. Changing time frames is one way to create depth to writing because it often conveys history, motivation and purpose.

Another: dialogue. Is it direct or indirect? Is it 'realistic'? Or 'stylised'? How is it paced? Is it 'interrupted' with e.g., views of how people look, how people think, what else is going on in the surroundings?

Another: when, where and how do we see, hear, smell, taste what is going on? Traditionally this is called 'descriptive writing'? What is it for? Does it add to or subtract from the action? Is it working to help us feel for the action and understand it, or does it feel like the author is grandstanding?

In non-fiction writing, there are often rule-bound forms to follow according to the place or purpose of the writing: newspaper sports report, opinion column, book/film/music review. Same goes for e.g., recipes, science experiments, accounts of a day out, re-telling of history, geography; representing one argument in favour or against something; representing several arguments in relation to each other. I've always been surprised by own children's homework how often they have had to do a piece of non-fiction writing without a model to look at first so that its method can be imitated. Starting from scratch, even with the cue questions that the teacher has provided have often felt that there isn't enough in the questions to get a feel of what's expected.

So these are all questions that we can ask when investigating and/ or imitating a piece of writing. I am suggesting that it's the writing (presumably by someone who is good at it) that is a crucial (if not the most important) teacher in this matter and the writing-teacher's job is to use the writing as a kind of template or trigger. Through a combination of investigating and imitating, 'the way writing works' offers a new or young writer a way in.

I've read quite a few 'this is how to write' books and more often than not, they are full of exercises, rules and directions rather than a much simpler approach which says, e.g., 'You could write like that' – in which 'like that' can mean, 'that way of writing', 'what that writing is about', 'what is triggered off by that piece of writing', a 'parody' of that way of writing. To my mind there is 'virtuous circle' made up of:

read ... think ... talk ... investigate ... imitate ... read ... think ... talk

... in which trying to, say, imitate the way of writing in question is a powerful way of investigating it in order to find out 'how it works'. In short, every kind of writing from any time or place is available to us to have a go at copying, in some fashion or another.

In the next section, I will add in 'invent' to the virtuous circle.

Part 6

Invention

By this I mean 'creative', 'innovative', 'new', 'original' and applies in this case to all kinds of writing, not just stories, poems and plays, and also applies to many other spheres of life and work: all the arts, applies arts, engineering, anything involving planning, figuring out a way forward mentally, visualising what to do in, say, sport or housing, politics and so on. My own view is that the fate of us on this planet depends on this, so anything that encourages, fosters and nurtures it in schools is to be welcomed. However, I think that it needs attention and loving care to ensure that pupils don't feel stressed or under-represented in the process. Invention, inventiveness, creativity and the like need time and space to breathe (it can't easily be jammed into short units overshadowed by the demands of learning outcomes and objectives) and they require 100% respect for everyone in an atmosphere of mutual nurture and co-operation.

Here is 'manifesto' for how we teach 'the arts' that I wrote some time ago:

We need to make sure that how we do the art is as important as the fact that we're doing it. After all, it's quite possible to do arts in education in ways which, say, undermine children. For instance, it's quite possible to be authoritarian and dictatorial while doing the arts – and more often than not this will teach children that they should just obey orders or that the arts are about being bossy or snooty.

Children and young people involved in the arts should:

1. have a sense of ownership and control in the process;

2. have a sense of possibility, transformation and change – that the process is not closed with pre-planned outcomes;

3. feel safe in the process, and know that no matter what they do, they will not be exposed to ridicule, relentless testing, or the fear of being wrong;

4. feel the process can be individual, co-operative or both;

5. feel there is a flow between the arts, that they are not boxed off from each other;

6. feel they are working in an environment that welcomes their home cultures, backgrounds, heritages and languages;

7. feel that what they are making or doing matters – that the activity has status within the school and beyond;

8. be encouraged and enabled to find audiences for their work;

9. be exposed to the best practice and the best practitioners possible;

10. be encouraged to think of the arts as including or involving investigation, invention, discovery, play and co-operation and to think that these happen within the actual doing, but also in the talk, commentary and critical dialogue that goes on around the activity itself.

As young people work, they will find their minds, bodies and materials changing. As agents of that change, they will inevitably change themselves. They will find out things about themselves as individuals – where they come from, how they co-exist with people and places around them – and they will pick up (or create) clues about where they are heading. They will also find new ways to talk about the arts. Demystifying them, if you like.

I believe that if we set out the stall for the arts in this way, we won't find ourselves trying to advocate a particular art form – say, painting – for what are deemed to be its intrinsic civilising qualities. Instead, we will be calling for a set of humane and democratic educational practices for which the arts provide an amenable home.

When it comes to writing in particular, I think it's best to see it as part of the continuum that I've been describing in the previous sections: collecting, investigating, imitating – and part of the continuum that I'll go on to describe. Isolating 'creativity' or 'invention' from these other activities and processes can lead to things drying up, or putting heavy demands on pupils to be 'imaginative' or 'original' without there being enough to be original with.

That said, here are two basic principles about invention in the sphere of writing – excuse the jargon – invention at the level of 'paradigm' or at the level of 'syntax' – or both.

Let me explain. Here's a sentence we all know: 'The cat sat on the mat'. It won't take you long to change any of those words into another, simply by taking out the word that's there, and replacing it with another, whilst sticking to that category of word.

You could change 'cat' to 'dog' or 'child' or 'dragon'.

You could change 'sat' to 'talked' or 'ran about'.

You could change 'on' to 'with'.

You could change 'mat' to 'table' or 'playground'.

These could all be 'paradigmatic' changes or, as some call it 'vertical' changes or as I sometimes call it, 'taking out one bit of Lego out of a Lego construction and putting another colour in'.

Now you could also change the structure, grammar or syntax of the sentence whilst keeping the cat, mat and the act of sitting the same. You could change singulars to plurals, you could change the verb 'sat' in many different ways ('was sitting', 'is going to sit', 'might have sat' etc.).

You could take things out: 'The cat sat.'

You could start adding things that describe the cat ('tabby'), tell us something about the verb: 'idly'. You could use phrases and clauses which add things to each part of the sentence: 'in the morning', 'when I walked into the room', 'that belonged to Kaya'.

You could also turn the statement into a question, or a command, or an exclamation; you could make it a 'negative'.

You could switch the sentence round so the 'mat' became the subject: 'The mat was sat on by the cat' and/or change the sequence in some way, (difficult to do when there is only one event, as with this sentence!).

All these are alterations at the 'syntagmatic' level.

I give this example, not so that you push children through an exercise as a virtue in itself, as is done by the requirements of the GPS test and the 'expected levels' of writing.

I give it in order to illustrate two main ways of change that we have available to us at every level of writing, not just at the sentence level. In other words, all pieces of writing have paradigms and syntax across the whole piece of writing. It's just that they're much easier to spot (and there is an agreed system) when it comes to sentences.

What do I mean?

Consider any genre of TV or film that you like. Let's say it's the talent show. What might we say are the paradigms? Perhaps we could say these are: contestants, competing, judges, judges comments, contestants' comments, contestants' family's comments, training sessions, live audiences, anchor-person/presenter, guest spot – and the setting: in the early rounds, some kind of rehearsal room, the final rounds a huge venue, and within that all the elements of lighting, sound, chairs, place at which the judges sit and so on.

What is the syntax?

At the singular-plural level – multiple contestants/judges/members of audiences/sometimes one or two presenters.

At the 'verb' level – the core 'verb' is 'they are competing', though there are 'clauses' where we have flashbacks to 'they were training' or 'they are visiting their home town and home itself' and of course, crucially, 'this is what has happened to me in my life' and 'this is what I hope for'.

At the sequence level, there is a sequence to – 'knock-out rounds one after the other', 'judges comments','contestants' comments' 'contestants' family's comments' , 'training sessions' etc.

Now, put yourself into the shoes of someone devising a new talent show. You can change the paradigms, the syntax of both.

Clearly, the easiest thing to change are the kinds of contestants. This is why someone like me muddles 'X-Factor' with 'Britain's Got Talent'. But consider another kind of talent show – the reality TV celebrity knock-out shows 'Big Brother' and 'Jungle'. Essentially, the big change there to start off with was at the paradigm level: they changed the setting.

Sticking with talent shows, go back to the list of paradigms and put yourself in the shoes of someone 'giving the show a shake-up' and you could change any of those in some way. The most major change would be to change the verb 'they are competing' to 'they are helping each other'!

Then again, you could change the syntax by, let's say, having only one judge; absurdly — reversing the sequence by starting with the crowning of the winner and working backwards! (Not so absurd when you think of the kinds of detective novels which begin by telling us whodunnit and the whole novel is about how the cops found out). You could create a sequence in the middle of the series in which the contestants judged the judges. (This is where the 'object' would swap places with the 'subject'.)

You can cut paradigms or add extra elements like, say: where all the contestants have to play a form of Masterchef at the half-way stage in the competition.

I won't go on.

You can apply this way of thinking to any form of writing: we can change the paradigms, the syntax or both. There's no need to be rigid about it, or get too hung up on which of the two is changing. In other words, we can do it intuitively, once we give ourselves the freedom to treat writing that already exists in this kind of a way — which is that it's our raw material on which to base new writing. And remember, this also includes the idea of 'importing' elements from one sphere into another (which is what I did with my 'Masterchef' proposal (!). This is the what is meant when writers or critics talk about 'using the motif of . . . ' or 'using the rhetorical devise of . . . '

What does all this mean for a writing activity (embedded within collecting, investigating, imitating — and later on we shall see in distribution/publication)?

The most obvious paradigms in fiction, poetry and plays are the answers to questions about where? when? who? how? or 'setting', 'time frame', 'characters/protagonists' 'what they are doing'. Those who thing 'structurally' about this kind of writing would also put elements like 'engendering empathy for the protagonists' 'engendering dislike of a protagonist', 'reveal-conceal', 'jeopardy/peril' 'the helping hand', the 'obstacle to fulfilment of the objective', the 'downbeat moment when things aren't going too well' etc., would make this sort of thing a necessary paradigm in say 'all feature films'.

In non-fiction, it's more diverse to be able to tie it down like this, but we might say, for example, with some kinds of non-fiction it's, 'the location of the piece of writing', 'the intended audience', 'the writer's personal opinion', 'references to other people's opinions', 'the use of examples/illustrations' but clearly, a recipe or a set of instructions on how to assemble a table would have a different set of paradigms.

Syntax for fiction, poetry and plays is a huge and fascinating subject and involve questions around plotting, managing of the audiences emotions (if that is possible!) through such processes of how writers create a sense of 'care' or 'empathy' in audience's minds for protagonists, problems for protagonists, peril and jeopardy.

They also involve crucial questions of sequencing, and on occasions turning singulars into plurals.

Consider for example, how the classic Western is usually singular but road movies are usually plural. Both could be changed if you so chose to.

And, as mentioned before, you can 'import' anything you want. It's often been noted that what J.K.Rowling did in the Harry Potter books was 'import' the 'school novel' into the 'fantasy novel' (or was it vice versa?!) Either way, she created what had formerly been seen as two distinct genres and made them into one. This created a huge syntactic melting point in which 'clauses' from one were latched on to 'clauses' in the other. Fantastic creatures were in school; big issues of world-threatening destiny were in school. And so on.

Now, to have described all this in the way that I've just done can make writing sound rather mechanical: just a matter of changing elements and processes, cutting things out, switching things round, adding stuff and so on . . . well, yes, kind of.

The job for anyone leading some writing is to keep the fun going. The core to this is to make it all an act of discovery: if we change x, what happens? (That is, what happens to the characters, what happens to the plot, what happens to – most important – the audience's expectations, feelings, predictions and sense of fulfilment (or not) at the end.)

We don't have to fake this, in that treating writing as an experiment, really does mean that we won't know what the effect is until we've done it.

So, all we have to do is start from a piece of writing, any piece of writing: fiction, plays, poems – non-fiction of any kind and say, 'What if we change this? What if we change that?' and then sit back and see what happens. The world of writing is out there to plunder, borrow from, scavenge from for us to change, mix and match, cut, add to, provide sequels and prequels for, dive into and pull out characters and ask them – what do you think? what do you want to do? where would you like to be? In non-fiction we can 'find out more about what x thinks', we can put x in contrast to y, and see what z says too. We can weigh up whether the examples do illustrate the argument – or not. Whether we need more or fewer. We can look at paragraphs and check whether they really do add to the overall argument or not. If not, why are they there? (There may be a good or bad reason.) If it's an account of an event or trip, what kind of detail attracts the most interest and which kind the least? Why is that? Does it have to be in chronological sequence or are there other sequences that might be better?

We can model any of these changes. We can demonstrate working some changes on a piece of writing. We can invite the invention by whoever is in the writing class and then by sharing our different inventions these become models too.

This 'apprenticeship' approach to writing doesn't suit all kinds of writing, nor should it be seen as the sole way to work. There are other occasions when we might want to make things more spontaneous, more free-flowing, more on impulse. We can, as I've shown elsewhere, sometimes start from another point: daydreaming, looking at a picture, doing a dance, doing an improv, watching a film, taking a walk, making something, having a discussion.

I would say that the two ways of kicking things off will inform each other: doing the collecting, imitating, inventing processes will inform the daydreaming-impulse writing; and the daydreaming-impulse writing will inform the imitating-inventing.

There is no need to be rigid about this. There is no need to think that one is superior to the other. There is great virtue in keeping things different, varied, changing and new. There is no virtue in keeping things the same every time. What works once or twice may not work the third time because it feels too 'used'.

Invention – Example

I thought it would be a good idea to take an actual example of a piece of literature where you could work the paradigm-syntax method of imitation.

Consider *The Tempest*.

If we construct a single sentence that is *The Tempest* we might get: 'A sorcerer-Duke gets revenge on the person who usurped him.'

We might add in some phrases with things like 'by using his powers to bring the usurper and his entourage to his island-home and to marry off his daughter with the usurper's son.'

We can add in the sub-plot with some clauses like 'while the native inhabitants (who the sorcerer Duke has enslaved) team up with the usurper's servants and stage a revolt that fails.'

So each noun and verb of this are the paradigms – any one, some or all of which we could change to create new versions of the story.

So 'island-home' could be, instead, a motel in the Nevada desert, where an ex-millionaire has holed up, having been cheated of his wealth by a partner. The 'native inhabitants' could be staff members at the motel who he keeps promising to pay but never gets round to it . . . and so on.

And we can change the syntax – altering e.g., singulars/plurals; sequencing; switching 'subjects and objects' (i.e., by switching who does what to whom); turn something that IS done into something that is NOT done; cutting some 'phrases and clauses' and/or adding others i.e., sub-plots; other 'conditions' in which more things take place and the like; changing 'modalities' – these are the auxiliary verbs that can express degree of certainty, degree of need, degree of possibility i.e., must, would, should, might, want, could. In fiction terms this is expressed by the degree to which people are or are not motivated to do things.

So, maybe we don't need two 'inhabitants' – maybe our ex-millionaire is a bit of a sleaze-ball and he has emotionally enslaved a woman. He keeps lying about how much money he has and how he is going to take her away somewhere.

Then, the guy who cheated him turns up at the motel, on the road with his son (perhaps we can junk the idea that he was lured there by magic) and some kind of person who works for him . . . a driver perhaps? Sleaze ball plots his revenge on cheat. Perhaps sleaze-ball has his son with him too and the revenge involves something he sets up with his son who lures the son of the guy who cheated him into some kind of jeopardy . . . gambling? (so sleaze-ball can get some money back) or more dangerous, so that he gets trapped in a forest somewhere?

Meanwhile, the woman that sleaze-ball has enslaved starts up something with driver-guy and they plot against sleaze-ball and/or the usurping-cheat guy.

This all feels like it's going to end badly, so a whole new syntax for the ending.

It feels like it's going to be a hostage situation/and or murder in which woman plus driver guy are going to relieve usurper guy of some money.

If that's the case then perhaps this whole thing needs to not start at the 'beginning'.

Perhaps we start the whole story with woman plus driver-guy running the motel and an inquisitive person (cop? journalist? writer? tax investigator) turns up and starts snooping around trying to find out how they came to be running the place. This takes us into a flashback so that we can then tell the story from the point at which the sleaze-ball is bossing the woman around and the cheating guy turns up . . . .

The potential with this 'new' story is that it can reveal something about relative moralities – the big crook(s) who are on the 'right' side of the law (sleaze-ball and cheat are not criminals, they simply try to eliminate each other) while the lower class commit a crime to come by their money.

Any piece of writing, fiction or non-fiction, poetry or drama can be changed using these principles.

Part 7

Distribution

An important, significant part of this whole process is what we do with whatever it is the pupils write. Traditionally, most of what is written goes into exercise books, which are sent to teachers who then mark them and hand them back. This means in terms of distribution this kind of writing only gets an audience of one, and that audience is not reading that piece for the prime reason of pleasure but of correcting it, and/or helping the writer develop/get better etc.

To be clear, there is nothing wrong per se with this, but there is a problem to my mind, if this is the main or only channel for helping a writer get better. Imagine instead, if we thought of a school which can behave most of the time as if it's a 'commissioning' body: it commissions writing from pupils so that it can be published and/or performed. The job of the school, then, would be to use as many different forms for the pupils' work as possible: on the print front that would include (as it does in many schools anyway) wall magazines, blogs, school bulletins, booklets, pamphlets, books in the library, books on sale at school fetes and parents' evenings. On the performance front that would include class performances and readings, performances by older to younger pupils and vice versa, whole school performances, parent-teacher-pupil joint performances, videos, PowerPoint with audio performances, talking books etc., and 'performance' could be made an important part of the informal curriculum so that it's studied.

Of course, under present conditions with so much testing, I realise that making this an objective is extremely hard. Yet where and when it happens, teachers can vouch for the fact that what is written ends up being read over and over again by other pupils (good for reading then!) and those who write have many reasons for 'getting things right' or 'improving the writing' – they want people to read and like what they read.

Performance has the power of interpretation on its side. With every act of preparing a piece for performance, the performer has to interpret what's been written. They have to decide on tone, rhythm, volume and movement and whether it does or does not fit the writing in question. This will involve talk and debate whether things are working right, and following performances, discussions can be focussed on what can we learn from each other, what did we see in that performance that we can try out ourselves.

The overall effect of seeing writing as a form of commissioning for publication and performance is that it starts to affect what is written, and how. Consider for example the strange fact that though film, TV and radio are massively important media for us in society, the curriculum downgrades or ignores the writing of scripts for performance. Why should, say, writing a story be any more important in status than writing a script of a story that is performed in front of an audience? Why is this sort of activity usually restricted to Christmas and end-of-year shows? If pupils are now writing stories and poems on computers, it's comparatively easy to turn these into blogs, online magazines and the like. There's no problem about restricting who can see these because there are always buttons which control this. This way an audience for the pupils' writing can be widened only so far as the school decides.

Again, in the area of non-fiction, this kind of written output can encourage the writing of reviews of books, films and song albums, reports of sports matches, school trips, debates and opinion columns.

As with all writing, there are ways to make these better and raise their status as important ways to write. In so doing, this kind of writing becomes much less abstract. There is a built-in need to interest audiences which invites debate about what makes for an interesting/exciting/funny report or review? This can take us back to examples in the press to imitate and use for invention.

This is what was always called 'writing for purpose'. The digital media have made it comparatively easy to achieve this. And there's an added educational dimension to this. We constantly hear from ministers and the Department for Education about how education is supposed to equipping pupils for their later lives. Part of that is surely using whatever means are available to us to publish and distribute. Our phones, tablets and computers are massively powerful ways for us to disseminate ideas and by using them in schools, we can show pupils of all ages that they can be used for many different ways of communicating with each other.

Crucial to all this, then is that we involve the pupils in the 'means of production' – that they are part of the process of making the books, audio, video, websites, blogs etc., so that they learn how to do that as part of the process of writing. Writing isn't just a matter of putting words on the page. It's a matter of making writing part of a loop that includes real readers and getting involved in questions about how we get the writing to the reader, does just this. Where some pupils may not want to perform their work, others can do that, and the non-performer can perhaps be more involved in the 'means of production' side, should that be appropriate.

This matter of 'distribution', then, helps us achieve the aim of creating reading-writers and writing-readers, or as I would add in: reading-performing-writers and writing-performing-readers.

Even if what I've described here is unrealisable across a whole year, perhaps it can be achieved in times when, say, the curriculum can be suspended for a day or a week, or a fortnight perhaps after SATs, or the like. We could think of, say, a publication-performance week and a whole school goes flat out in getting all these different things made, done and 'out there'. Why not?

Part 8

What have I left out?

It's easy when writing things like this to tie everything up into neat programmes or lists of things to do. I've tried to make clear throughout that whatever I've written here and elsewhere they are for adapting by whoever is reading it.

There's another aspect to this: there are always bits missed out, an emphasis that was skewed, points that were not made, so this last section is a kind of rag-bag of thoughts about what comes before.

1. All writing is helped by reading. The more that pupils read, the easier it is for them to write. The more widely they read, the easier it is for them to write. This is no mystery: writing involves us assembling words and structures in the writing-way-of-doing-language. By reading, we put into our heads the structures that belong to writing. We use these in order to write. This means that any way in which we can get every pupil reading for pleasure is a fantastic way to improve writing. There are now online and in books many suggestions for how to carry out a whole school policy on reading for pleasure.

2. Much of what I've written here has put forward suggestions for 'processes' in which the process in question has been 'structured'. Only occasionally, have I dispensed with that and suggested freer ways of writing. I don't want to minimise this. When you have a group who are reading a lot, talking about what they're reading, and, say, performing poems or reading each other's stories, there'll be plenty of times when all we need to do is provide an open trigger or stimulus: a piece of music, a clip from a film, a walk in the snow. There'll be times in the midst of production of a magazine, when the need of the moment – to have a write-up of that netball game, to have a review of the latest album by 'x', and that job has to be done straightaway. These much more spontaneous ways of producing writing are no less valid than any of the more structured ones that I've suggested. What's more, the methods of one can feed into the other. Any writer will tell you, that part of writing is to have moments of 'inspiration' that arise out of daydreaming, walking, looking out of the window, and other parts come from having to write for a deadline, taking instructions from editors about what to take out and what to put in (often based on the expectations of genre – a form of modelling, if you like – imitation-invention!). We need both.

3. The different sections of this booklet are intended to be influencing and affecting each other: collecting, investigating, imitating, inventing and distributing. In any given day or week or year, it's not that one should come before another. The idea is that are all going on simultaneously: informing and helping each other.

4. You can take any part of this booklet – or all of it – and use it for school-based research. You can think of any part of it as an 'intervention' and you can observe/analyse yourself teaching it, observe/analyse the pupils responding to that intervention, observe/analyse the writing that comes out of it, observe/analyse other teachers', parents' reactions to the outcomes. This is what we do at Goldsmiths in our term 'Children's Literature in Action' as part of our MA in Children's Literature. I supervise teachers, librarians or people working in arts and education doing these kinds of studies. The 'matrix' in my booklet *Poetry and Stories for Primary and Lower Secondary Schools* is for teachers to use as a way of analysing pupils' responses to literature. I would recommend anyone reading this booklet and trying out any of the ideas to set up some kind of research or monitoring arrangement. Everyone involved will benefit from such work.

5. Some of the best work I've seen has arisen from 'whole school texts'. This is where a staff agree on a text that can work for the whole school to interpret in different ways: to read, discuss, investigate, write responses to, stories around, reviews, make videos, do art work, look at the history of the writer and/or work and/or culture it came from. I saw Ranelagh School in Newham do this with *The Tempest* and there was work from nursery to Year 6 on this taking episodes and scenes from the play, modern versions writing their own, doing performances, paintings, building islands and so on. And the children were sharing their work with each other and with parents.

You might be interested in my book, *What is Poetry? An Essential Guide to Reading and Writing Poetry* published by Walker Books.

I often post thoughts on education, literature, and current affairs on my blog at: michaelrosenblog.blogspot.co.uk

You can also follow my work at: michaelrosen.co.uk

CPSIA information can be obtained
at www.ICGtesting.com
Printed in the USA
BVHW030738091220
595258BV00002B/252